Children

Second World War

Children in a trench dug across a park and used as a simple bomb shelter.

Dr Brian Knapp

"This morning the British Ambassador in Berlin handed the German government a final note stating that unless we heard from them by 11 o'clock, that they were prepared at once to withdraw their troops from Poland, a state of war would exist between us. I have to tell you now that no such undertaking has been received and that consequently this country is at war with Germany."

Neville Chamberlain,
Prime Minister, 3 September 1939

▲ VE-Day, when huge numbers of people gathered outside Buckingham Palace, London.

Curriculum Visions

There's much more on-line including videos

You will find multimedia resources covering the Second World War and many more history, science, geography, religion and spelling subjects in the Professional Zone at:

www.CurriculumVisions.com

A CVP Book
Copyright Earthscape © 2007

First reprint 2007

The right of Brian Knapp to be identified as the author of this work has been asserted by him in accordance with the Copyright, Designs and Patents Act 1988.

Author
Brian Knapp, BSc, PhD

Senior Designer
Adele Humphries, BA, PGCE

Editors
Jan Smith (former Deputy Head of Wellfield School, Burnley, Lancashire) and Gillian Gatehouse

Designed and produced by
EARTHSCAPE

Printed in China by
WKT Company Ltd

Children in the Second World War – *Curriculum Visions*
A CIP record for this book is available from the British Library

Paperback ISBN 978 1 86214 228 2
Hardback ISBN 978 1 86214 229 9

Illustrations
David Woodroffe

Picture credits
All photographs are from the Earthscape Picture Library except the following: (c=centre t=top b=bottom l=left r=right)
Corbis pages 6t, 10–11, 16, 20, 21, 22b, 23, 24–25, 38, 42, 43; *Glamorgan Archives* pages 18–19; *A friend of the Dilke Memorial Hospital* pages 30–31; *The Granger Collection, New York* pages 17, 27; *The Illustrated London News* pages 6bl, 14–15, 29; *Imperial War Museum* pages 18tl, 32, 36–37, 37, 40–41; *Library of Congress* cover and pages 1, 2, 13br, 44c, 46–47; *The National Archives* pages 22t, 28, 45; *ShutterStock* pages 5, 12–13 (Spitfire), 12c, 39. *The publishers have made their best endeavours to contact all copyright holders for material published in this book.*

This product is manufactured from sustainable managed forests. For every tree cut down at least one more is planted.

Contents

Note: in this book the term 'Britain' is used as a shorthand, meaning "The United Kingdom of Great Britain and Northern Ireland".

Words in **BOLD CAPITALS** are further explained in the glossary on pages 46 and 47.

▲ A cross remembering those who fell during the world wars.

What was the Second World War?

The Second World War affected many countries in the world. A group of countries – Germany, Italy and Japan – fought the allied countries (ALLIES) of Britain, its Commonwealth partners and the USA.

War – it's one of the most terrifying words in any language, yet it has happened in every century since records began. Many of these wars happened a long time ago and may not seem real to us.

However, the Second World War (World War II) is different (picture ①). Your grandparents may have been alive during or just after this war and can still tell you of their memories.

Britain and allies
Germany and allies
Controlled by Germany and allies
Neutral

▼ ① Areas controlled by the warring nations in the early days of the war.

Norway
Finland
Estonia
Sweden
Latvia
Denmark
Lithuania
Ireland
Soviet Union
Great Britain
Netherlands
Poland
Belgium
Germany
Czechoslovakia
France
Switzerland
Austria
Hungary
Romania
Yugoslavia
Portugal
Bulgaria
Spain
Italy
Sardinia
Albania
Corsica
Turkey
Greece
Morocco
Algeria
Malta
Cyprus
Tunisia
Libya
Egypt

▲ ② **Remembrance Day (11 November) is a special day when we remember men and women killed during the two World Wars and other conflicts.**

If you look around, you may think there are few signs of the Second World War. There are MEMORIALS, of course (picture ② and pages 3, 8 and 9). But is there anything else? In fact, many of the huge changes that have happened to Britain in recent years were brought about by that war.

In this book you will find out what it was like to be in the war, and you will find hints as to why life after the war has never been the same.

Why did the war start?

No wars start for simple reasons. Usually they start because of things that had been happening for a long time.

Some of the causes of World War II can be found in World War I, that ended 25 years earlier. At the end of that war, in 1918, Germany signed a peace treaty which the German people thought was very unfair.

For years after World War I, the Germans had little to eat, few jobs and they felt they had lost their pride and honour. This was a dangerous time because they could easily be persuaded by unscrupulous people that there was honour, glory and a better life ahead. After all, what could be worse?

► ① A class being taught about Hitler in 1939.

▼ ② Adolf Hitler was one of the worst dictators the world has ever known. Yet he was able to portray himself to Germans as a kindly father figure, as this picture shows.

The Nazi party

This was how a small, extreme party was able to come to power. It was called the National Socialist Party, which came to be known as the NAZI Party. Its ruthless leader was Adolf Hitler (pictures ① and ②).

Hitler was a very powerful speaker and his speeches persuaded people to believe in him as their leader. Away from the public eye he was ruthless and had no problem in killing people to take control of the Nazi Party.

Second World War timeline

	3 Sept: War with Germany begins	Meat rationing begins	Bacon, butter and sugar rationed	Home Guard created	Battle of Britain begins	Dec 1941: USA enters the war

1938   **1939**   **1940**   **1941**

Gas masks issued   Evacuation of children begins   **The Phoney War**   Winston Churchill becomes Prime Minister   Blitz begins   Blitz ends in failure for Germany

By 1933, public charm and private treachery had moved him into the most powerful position in Germany. Soon he became the military **DICTATOR** of the country.

People followed him because his policies started to provide more jobs and made people better off. He rebuilt the German army and this gave the Germans pride.

He then told people that they needed more living space and they simply had no alternative but to take it, just as peoples had done in the past. This meant invading Germany's neighbours. As a result, war came ever closer.

The Nazis' dark side

The Nazis were very skilled at getting their message across. This is called **PROPAGANDA** (and in modern times, 'spin'). What they said was not always the truth.

The dark side of the Nazis was truly horrible, with Jews, gypsies and many other people being rounded up and put into **CONCENTRATION CAMPS** and killed. But somehow the German people did not wake up to this.

Germany over-runs Europe

Hitler was a bold planner. He pushed and pushed against the rules of the peace treaty and the other European countries did nothing to stop him.

In Britain, the Prime Minister, Neville Chamberlain, was a very good man, but for the times he was too weak. As a result, Adolf Hitler was able to re-arm and take over other countries, while Britain – then one of the most powerful countries in the world – stood by. At the same time the United States did not want to be involved in another war and so they stood idly by, too.

Soon, Germany made agreements with other bad governments, such as Italy, Russia and Japan.

War with Britain begins

Britain had agreed to protect Poland. So when Germany invaded Poland on 3 September 1939, Neville Chamberlain was forced to declare war on Germany. Because Germany was allied with countries such as Italy and Japan, and because Britain had colonies across the world, this meant that this war was a World War.

Britain begins to win the war in North Africa

Allied troops invade Italy

Germany fires the first rocket bombs at Britain

Hitler commits suicide

Some rationing stops

1943   **1944**   **1945**   **1946**

Allied invasion of France from Britain (called D-Day)

VE-Day to mark the end of war in Europe

Rationing not over until 1954

Why we have memorials

We have memorials to remind us of the sacrifice many people made in every corner of the country, and how tragic war can be.

World War II lasted six long years – from 1939 to 1945. It affected everyone in Britain, but also in the nations connected to Britain. Many of the Commonwealth countries (such as Singapore and Malaya) were overrun by the Japanese and many others countries (such as Australia, Canada, India and New Zealand) willingly sent troops to help make the world a better and safer place.

Memorials

Wherever you go in the Commonwealth you will find war **MEMORIALS** (pictures ① and ②). In Britain there is one in every parish and borough. If you look at them you will see the names of people who went to fight in the war and who never came back because they were killed in action.

▼ ① These are names on a memorial. Read your local memorials and try to find out something about at least one of the people who used to live near to you.

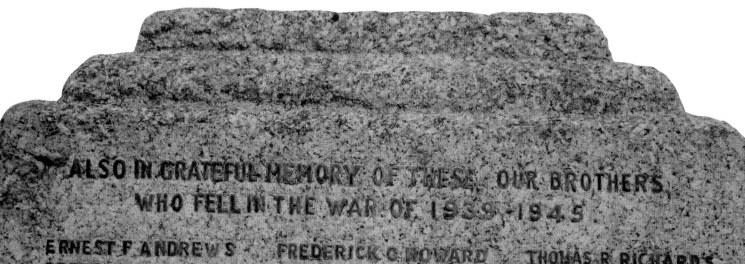

ALSO IN GRATEFUL MEMORY OF THESE OUR BROTHERS
WHO FELL IN THE WAR OF 1939-1945

ERNEST F ANDREWS
PETER F BEARD
JOHN M BLANDY
LAWRENCE C CRANE
ALLAN A FORD
SPENCER C FORD
JOHN D HAYES
HORACE A HOLMANS
ERNEST RAINEY

FREDERICK C HOWARD
PERCY JACKMAN
ALFRED R JENKINS
CECIL RYDEE
RUSSELL MARTIN
HENRY O PHILLIPS
WILLIAM POSTLETHWAITE
CYRIL C BRISTOW

THOMAS R RICHARDS
ANTONY P TOMKINSON
ERIC TUBB
WILLIAM J WALTERS
WILLIAM WARD
ROBERT A WEBSTER
NATHANIEL J WHEELER
PETER WHITE
FRANK C MASON

▲ ② Many war memorials are in churchyards. The British national war memorial (the cenotaph) is in Whitehall near the Houses of Parliament.

Lost relatives

These people were someone's sons or brothers. But above all, many were fathers. A child who lived in the parish or borough may never again see their father, and would grow up after the war with a small corner of their world forever sad.

So the war affected children as well as adults.

Each year the nation remembers the people who died in the war (and those of other wars). Even though World War II ended over 60 years ago, the events leading up to the war, and the war itself, must never be forgotten, so that dreadful events like this should never be allowed to happen again.

Weblink: www.CurriculumVisions.com

The Battle of Britain

Because Britain is an island, the German army could not invade easily. So they began a bombing campaign.

The Germans had thought up a new kind of war. They used tanks (panzers) and bomb-carrying planes (picture ①).

This new fast attack was meant to end any war quickly. In fact, the Germans planned to conquer many parts of Europe in just a few weeks. This new kind of fast war was called Blitzkrieg in German (in English it is 'lightning war').

The German Blitzkrieg plan worked well. In a year Belgium, France, the Netherlands, Denmark and Norway were all defeated. This left Britain to stand alone against the might of Hitler's Germany.

Why Britain was special

To conquer Britain, you have to invade by sea. Britain had the world's most powerful navy, far bigger than Germany's. But most important of all, Britain also had an airforce.

◀ ① A rally in a German stadium is overflown by part of the huge German airforce. The flags show the Nazi Party swastika.

If the Germans tried to send over soldiers in ships, they could easily be destroyed by British aircraft.

So the Germans realised they needed to destroy the British air force before they could invade.

So, for Britain, the first stage of the Blitzkrieg attack was to bomb British airfields.

German air power

The Germans had a vast fleet of fighter and bomber aircraft. The British had not kept up.

11

The British had brilliant engineers who eventually made planes better than the Germans – the Spitfire (picture ②) and the Hurricane are still remembered across the world.

But it took time before the British government started to re-arm. By the start of war, the air force only had a quarter of the planes that the Germans had (640 compared to 2,500).

▼ ② The famous British Spitfire fighter plane.

The Blitzkrieg

In July 1940 bombing began with attacks on British airfields, aircraft factories and **RADAR** stations. Hitler wanted to destroy the Royal Air Force (RAF) while it was on the ground.

▼▶ ③ Just in case the Germans invaded, the British government set up many defensive gunsites. Because of their shape – low and round – they became nicknamed 'pillboxes'. Each had a gun trained on the most likely route the Germans would use.

Many pillboxes still survive in the countryside and you can visit them.

► ④ Germans made up this picture from two pictures, one of a plane, the other of London docks. It was never a real picture. This is an example of Nazi propaganda. They wanted their own people to see that Germany had control of the skies. In reality it did not.

The RAF commanders sent up **FIGHTER PLANES** to attack. With skill and determination they were able to shoot down large numbers of German planes (picture ④). This time was known as the Battle of Britain and the British fighters won (picture ⑤).

It was after this that the new Prime Minister, Winston Churchill, (picture ⑥) made his famous speech in which he declared:

> "*Never in the field of human conflict was so much owed by so many to so few.*"

It was nothing short of the truth.

► ⑤ A poster celebrating Britain's achievements in the Battle of Britain.

LET'S GO-

WINGS FOR VICTORY

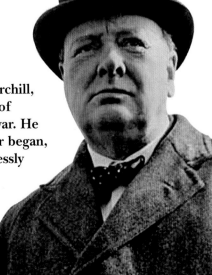

► ⑥ Winston Churchill, the Prime Minister of Britain during the war. He was 65 when the war began, but he worked tirelessly year after year.

The Blitz begins

The Blitz was a time when German planes bombed British cities in an effort to make the British people surrender.

Hitler did not know the strength and reserves of the RAF. In fact, the RAF were just on the edge of being defeated because they were so outnumbered. But, as he did not know this, Hitler thought that he had to find another way of defeating Britain.

As it happened, a chance event was to trigger what Hitler did next. On 24 August 1940 a lost German bomber crew accidentally bombed London instead of the airfields it had been given as a target. Prime Minister, Winston Churchill, thought the Germans had meant to attack London, so he told the RAF to bomb Berlin, the capital of Germany.

Hitler was shocked by the attack on his homeland. In a furious speech he said:

"If they send over a hundred bombers to bomb our cities, then we shall send a thousand planes to bomb theirs. And if they think that they can destroy our cities, then we shall wipe theirs from the face of the Earth."

▲ ① This map shows where bombs (●) fell on just one small area of Glasgow. It shows you how much effect bombing had.

In a rage, Hitler ordered the German air force (the Luftwaffe) to stop attacking airfields and to attack ports and cities instead. He thought that bombing the people would make them want to ask for peace.

In fact, it had just the opposite effect. It also gave precious time for the RAF to recover and, in the long run, beat the Germans back from British skies. But that would take many months.

▼ ② This was the centre of Coventry after the night raid of 14 November 1940. The ancient cathedral and much of the city centre were destroyed.

The Blitz

The bombing of cities was the start of the time called the Blitz (the word Blitz is a shortened version of Blitzkrieg, see page 10).

The Blitz affected nearly all major cities. From early September 1940 London was attacked on 57 nights in a row and over a million bombs were dropped.

Many other important industrial cities also suffered. The whole centre of Coventry was destroyed on one fateful night (picture ②). Glasgow suffered the worst because it was so important as a centre for making ships and weapons (picture ①).

Bombing was inaccurate, so even if the targets were meant to be docks, factories and railway lines, many bombs fell on nearby houses, shelters and hospitals. As a result, over 41,000 civilians were killed during the Blitz.

Weblink: www.CurriculumVisions.com

Tracking the bombers

In those days, planes flew at less than 200 miles an hour (300 km/hr). It is about 70 miles (110 km) from the south coast to London, so planes coming from Germany on bombing runs would take half an hour to reach the city.

A special wireless detecting system called **RADAR** could pick them up as they started across the Channel. Those keeping watch at the coast could also telephone ahead to give **AIR-RAID WARDENS** some warning of an **AIR RAID** and tell them how many planes were involved.

In each city, a system of air-raid sirens was set up to warn people of the raid and give them time to take cover. At the same time the anti-aircraft (known as **ACK-ACK**) gun crews were told to get ready to fire on the planes as they passed overhead.

Huge barrage balloons were flown above each city (picture ③). The thick steel tethering wires made flying difficult because if a plane flew into one, the wire could cut a wing off.

Seeing an air raid

Imagine seeing the first ever wave of bombers arriving over London at about four o'clock in the afternoon of 7 September 1940. It must have been a very frightening sight.

In the sky you would have seen 340 bombers protected by 600 fighters. Their target was the docks of London and their purpose was to drop hundreds of fire bombs (see page 18) and set the docks ablaze.

There were so many planes lining up to bomb London that it took them two hours to drop their bombs.

▼ ③ Barrage balloons being raised before the start of an air raid.

Blackout

Britain depends on its docks, its shipyards and the railways and roads that carry goods from the docks to where they are needed. This is why the Germans tried to bomb port cities such as Bristol, Glasgow, Liverpool, London and Plymouth.

It is easy to pick out cities at night by their lights. It is almost like having a map to aim with.

The only answer was to have a blackout, meaning that no-one was allowed to have a light showing at night. Heavy curtains or shutters had to be placed at windows (picture ④), car headlights were fitted with special hoods so they only shone downwards, and all street lights and shop lights were turned out. Cities were therefore totally black at night.

To make sure people obeyed this instruction, blackout wardens patrolled the streets.

▲ ④ Shutters being put up on a shop window just before the blackout.

The raid continues by night

This was not the end. The first bombs caused fires and as the fires raged they made beacons of light for the night bombers. They arrived about 8 o'clock in the evening. Their raid lasted even longer – it was not until 4.30 in the morning that the last bombs were dropped and the all-clear siren was sounded.

This first day was just the beginning of one of the most horrific periods of the war for the people of Britain's cities. The Blitz lasted for nine months. During this time there was hardly a night when the air-raid sirens did not wail or that the whine of bombs and their explosions could not be heard over one of Britain's cities.

By mid-October (just a month after the start of the Blitz) there were 250,000 people homeless in London alone due to the Blitz. This meant that there was a serious problem in finding shelter for all of them.

The last raid

On 10 May 1941 a 550 bomber raid dropped more than 700 tonnes of bombs and thousands of incendiaries (fire bombs). This was probably the worst raid of the Blitz with nearly 1,500 men, women and children killed in one day. But it was also the last of the mass raids. Hitler had turned his attention towards Russia. The bombing of British cities had been a failure.

What bombs did

Bombs were the main way that Germans attacked Britain.

▼ ① A 'doodlebug' (V1 rocket).

Bombs are metal tubes packed with explosives. They are made so that one end is heavier than the other. When they are dropped from aircraft (picture ①), they fall heavy-end down so that a firing device in the nose, called a detonator, will hit the ground and set off the explosive in the bomb.

Blast bombs

There are two kinds of bomb. The most common kind is called a blast bomb. The explosive breaks up the metal case and pieces of metal – called shrapnel – are thrown in every direction. The explosive also sends out shock waves that destroy buildings (picture ②). In World War II the bombs were generally only powerful enough to knock down one house at a time.

Bombs were dropped from planes in groups, known as 'sticks'. The bombs fell in a line, each separated by a few hundred metres. The result was a trail of damage from each plane.

▲ ② Bombing destroyed some buildings completely, but it also caused damage over a wider area. Look, for example, how many houses have been destroyed in this picture (Swansea) and the burned out roof of the church.

▶ ③ Once the raid was over, people went back to their houses to see what was left, and, if their house had been destroyed, to collect anything that was left.

▼ ④ Night-time bombing with incendiary bombs left a trail of burning buildings that were like beacons for the aircraft still waiting to drop their bombs.

Fire bombs

Fire (incendiary) bombs were often the most damaging. They were packed with a mixture of explosive and chemicals that caught fire as the bomb exploded. Burning explosive was scattered over a wide area, setting buildings alight (pictures ③ and ④).

Once a fire had started it was difficult to put it out during an air raid because water pipes were often damaged. Firefighters in wartime cities were among the most heroic of the cities' people (picture ⑤).

▼ ⑤ People were not demoralised by the bombing. If the shop was bombed out, people continued to sell their goods from a barrow in the road.

Weblink: www.CurriculumVisions.com

Finding shelter

Some people used underground railway stations. Others built shelters in their gardens. Some people did not bother with protection at all.

What could people do to protect themselves from the bombs? They could hope that the RAF fighters would attack the bombers before they arrived overhead; they could give early warnings using sirens, and defend with ack-ack guns; they could dig bombproof shelters; and, most dramatically of all, they could evacuate people from cities.

LOOK before you sleep

ALL WINDOWS AND INNER DOORS OPEN?

WATER IN BUCKETS?

WATER WATER

SAND SAND

SAND IN BUCKETS?

GAS MASK, CLOTHES AND TORCH HANDY?

GOOD NIGHT!

◀ ① **This poster told people how to be prepared for a nearby bomb hit.**

▶ ② **Many children were not evacuated and they stayed with their parents. When the bombs came they went to shelters, or they went down to the cellar of their house. Here is a (working CLASS) grandmother and children in a cellar. Look carefully at their clothes, how they are washing themselves and what is in the background.**

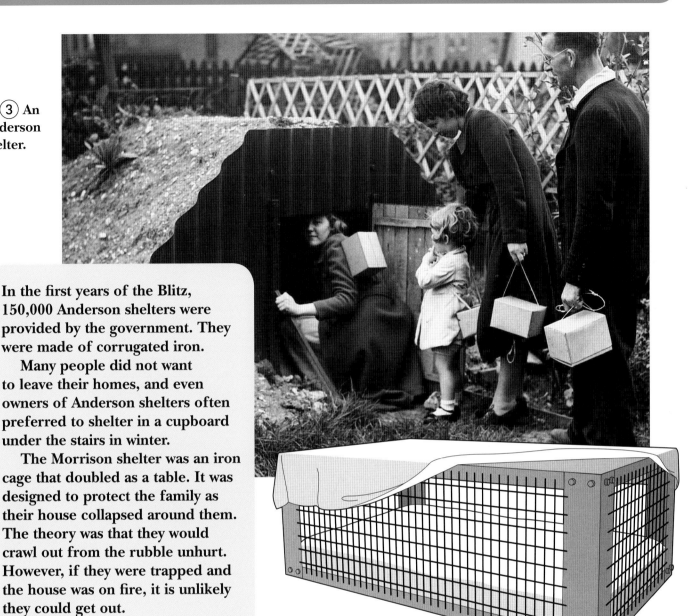

▶ ③ An Anderson shelter.

In the first years of the Blitz, 150,000 Anderson shelters were provided by the government. They were made of corrugated iron.

Many people did not want to leave their homes, and even owners of Anderson shelters often preferred to shelter in a cupboard under the stairs in winter.

The Morrison shelter was an iron cage that doubled as a table. It was designed to protect the family as their house collapsed around them. The theory was that they would crawl out from the rubble unhurt. However, if they were trapped and the house was on fire, it is unlikely they could get out.

▶ ④ A Morrison shelter.

Shelters

Making bombproof shelters was difficult. To be truly bomb-proof, the shelter has to be a deep 'cave' with a reinforced concrete roof. So few were ever built. But protection could be simple. Trenches were dug in parks (away from where buildings might collapse or fires take hold) and bricked over. They gave protection from shrapnel and were safe unless there was a direct hit on the trench.

Even so, many people decided to take their chances at home (pictures ① and ②). Those with deep cellars could use those. Those with gardens were encouraged to build their own shelters, or they could even build a shelter in their living room. Each type of shelter was named after its designer – the Anderson (picture ③) and the Morrison shelters (picture ④).

For those who wanted to escape the cities, special trains were run to places in the countryside. For example, trains ran from London every night to Kent where people would sleep in caves. But these could only hold a few people.

Shelters were also needed for important factories. As well as being used as a bomb shelter (picture ⑤), some parts of the London Underground were used as factories. They were closed off from trains and the tracks concreted over. Plessey's of Ilford, for example, which supplied the RAF with aircraft parts, became a tubular factory almost 5 miles (8 km) long, employing 2,000 workers.

▼ ⑤ As German planes flew overhead, dropping their sticks of bombs, some Londoners chose to go down into the Underground system. Some slept there all night. Many, however, found them noisy and smelly and preferred to take their chances at home.

In November 1940:
- 4% were sheltering in the Underground system.
- 9% in public shelters.
- 27% in domestic shelters, such as Anderson and/or Morrison shelters. Yet 60% of Londoners still preferred to stay in their own homes, sheltering mostly in cellars, underneath stairs, or even in cupboards.

Gas masks

In World War I many soldiers had been killed and injured by poison gas released over the battlefields. As World War II approached there was real fear that poison gas might be dropped from bombs. As a result, in 1938, the government decided that everyone should be issued with a gas mask (picture ⑥) and that they must carry it at all times.

Gas masks came in many shapes and sizes. There were 'Mickey Mouse' gas masks to help younger children think they were fun. Many children discovered the design meant that it accidentally produced a 'raspberry' noise, every time they breathed through it!

Civil Defence workers had a gas mask in green. Ordinary adult gas masks were black. They were a simple rubber mask, with a plastic visor and webbing to hold it on to the head. Gas masks were even made for horses and dogs!

◀ ⑥ A 'tin' (plated steel) helmet and gas mask were issued to wardens who had to be out during an air raid.

Why were children evacuated?

People worried that many children would be killed if they stayed near the docks. So plans were made to move them to the safety of the countryside.

The government believed that there might be millions of deaths from bombing, and so in the first few days of September 1939 they planned to move a million children and their teachers (who became their guardians) from places near docks and railways where they might get bombed, to the safety of towns and villages in the countryside. This movement was called evacuation and it was known as 'Operation Pied Piper'.

It did not involve children who lived in the outer parts of cities (the suburbs) where bombs rarely fell.

Many children were not told exactly what was going to happen. Quite often they were simply told they were going on holiday with their school for a few days (picture ①).

▼ ① Young children were lined up and labels put on them, saying who they were and where they were going. They became human parcels.

▲ ② Children were escorted in long 'crocodiles' to waiting buses.

Billeting

It was a huge problem trying to find new homes for such enormous numbers of children and then getting them from their own homes to their new destination.

A count was made of all of the spare rooms in every house in countryside villages. These were to be used as homes (**BILLETS**) for the evacuees. The process was compulsory: if you had spare rooms, you got evacuees, and you had no idea who they were and where they were coming from. It was all in the hands of a local official called a billeting officer.

Packed off like parcels

Smaller children could not understand what they were doing and there was a danger that they might get lost.

So each was treated just like a piece of luggage. Each child carried a gas mask in a box, some food and a change of clothing. They wore three labels saying who they were, where they had come from and where they were going to. Then they were told "Don't suck or eat your labels!".

Crocodiles

From the school they walked in 'crocodiles' or went in coaches with their teachers to the railway station (picture ②). Here they found themselves among tens of thousands of other children. Some thought it was all noisy and confusing, while others thought it was an exciting adventure.

When the children arrived at their destination there were often not enough spaces for them and so some local people had to take more children than they were expecting (picture ④). In many cases billeting officers lined the children up in a village and asked local people to take their pick. Many children heard "I'll take that one," and then found themselves whisked off – to the unknown.

A member of the family?

In the best billets, the new arrivals were treated like a member of the family, very often moving into homes much wealthier than they had been used to. In the worst, children were mistreated by families who didn't want them and didn't care about them.

Some were children newly arrived in England. These were mainly Jewish children who had just escaped from Germany or other European countries and now they had to be evacuated again away from their parents.

Freda Skrzypee, aged nine, who arrived with her parents and brother from Danzig on Sunday was among them. She spoke no English, but had a companion in Ruth Rosenzweig, a Jewish refugee from Berlin. "The Germans have taken away our nationality," she said, "But I am happy here." (*Daily Mirror*, 1939)

Evacuation overseas

The government also arranged for children to be sent to the USA,

Reasons to evacuate

You might get killed by bombs.
Your house might get bombed and then you would have nowhere to live.
Your city school might be closed and you would have nowhere to learn.
You would go to the countryside where you could learn in a school as normal.

▶ ③ A poster issued after evacuation warning mothers not to bring their children back from the countryside.

Reasons not to evacuate

You might end up with a family you didn't like or who didn't like you.
You might get separated from your friends.
You would be separated from your mother.
The chances of being killed by a bomb were not as great as some people feared.
You would not be able to take much with you.

Canada and Australia. In the first few months over 210,000 were registered with the scheme. However, one of the evacuation ships was sunk by a German **TORPEDO** and 73 children were killed, so the overseas evacuation stopped.

Did evacuation work?

When war was first declared, the evacuation plan was immediately put into effect. It was voluntary and about a sixth of all those who could leave did not want to go. Then for many months there were no bombing raids. This was a time called 'The Phoney War' and so some parents thought it would be safe for their children to come back home.

Many children were also homesick. By January 1940 nearly half of all evacuated schoolchildren had returned home (picture ③). It was then that the bombing began. In the long run, it was a lot of effort and it is doubtful if it saved many lives.

What was it like for billeting families?

Remember that the children evacuated were mostly from inner city areas near docks and factories. Most were from very poor families whose contact with the world beyond their own small area was almost non-existent. There wasn't the TV to watch as there is today and few people from these areas could afford a radio. Many had hygiene standards that would shock us today.

So if it was strange for the evacuated children to go out into the countryside, when many had never seen the countryside before in their lives, it was equally strange for those watching the children arrive.

Many country people were shocked to find that half of the children coming to them were dirty, and had fleas or head lice. At that time many houses in the poorest inner city areas still did not have toilets and children were used to going to the toilet wherever they felt like it – including public places.

▲ ④ Evacuated children lining up to have their bath in front of the kitchen stove (called a range).

The Home Guard

With most of the ABLE-BODIED men away in the forces, the British government had to think of ways to protect the country in case of attack. This was how the Home Guard came about.

The government had to find some way of defending Britain when most of the forces were fighting overseas. The answer was to make a force out of those who were in essential jobs, the elderly and those a bit too young to join the forces. This was soon known as the Home Guard (picture ①).

No weapons

By the end of June 1940, there were nearly 1.5 million volunteers, but to begin with they didn't even have uniforms, just an armband that said 'LDV' (Local Defence Volunteers). They had almost no weapons, for the weapons were going to the regular troops. So they made up for this by training to observe and report any enemy movements.

To counter the threat of an airborne or coastal attack, the Home Guard manned observation posts. Home guards spent every night watching the skies and the sea, often armed with no more than a cup of tea and a pitchfork.

▼ ① A Home Guard recruitment poster telling people what a vital task they would perform.

ARE **YOU** PREPARED FOR THIS ? IF NOT, THEN JOIN YOUR LOCAL HOME GUARD

Patrols were also carried out on foot, by bicycle, even on horseback. It was not until 1943 that the Home Guard became a well equipped and trained force (picture ②).

The Home Guard were formally disbanded on 3 December 1944, six months after the invasion of Europe had begun.

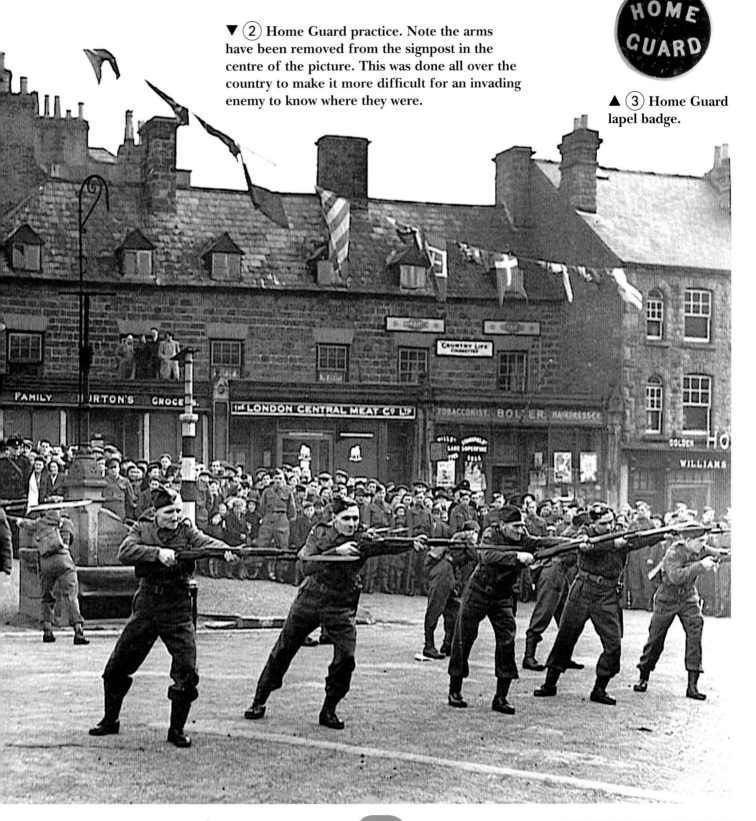

▼ ② Home Guard practice. Note the arms have been removed from the signpost in the centre of the picture. This was done all over the country to make it more difficult for an invading enemy to know where they were.

▲ ③ Home Guard lapel badge.

▲ ① Setting off depth charges (underwater bombs) over an area where a German submarine had been detected.

Why food became scarce

Britain cannot grow enough food to feed its people, so when war broke out and ships could not reach Britain easily, food had to be rationed.

Britain is a small country with many people. It cannot grow enough food from its own land and must get the extra food needed from overseas.

By the start of World War II, Britain was importing large amounts of wheat from the United States of America and Canada.

Other foods that were imported included cheese and butter (from Australia and New Zealand) tea (from India), coffee (from Brazil), sugar (from the West Indies) and many kinds of fruit.

Food was not the only thing that had to come from overseas. Some of these vital items were petrol (from the Middle East), wood and rubber (for car tyres, from Malaya).

The Battle of the Atlantic

One of the ways the Germans believed they could beat the British was to stop these vital supplies from arriving in Britain.

As a result they sent out their battleships and submarine fleet (U-boats) to hunt down and destroy the ships carrying supplies to Britain across the Atlantic.

The Prime Minister, Winston Churchill, wrote,

"... the only thing that ever really frightened me during the war was the U-boat (Unterseeboot) peril."

The Royal Navy organised the **MERCHANT SHIPS** into groups, called convoys, which they tried to protect with destroyers, cruisers and other naval vessels.

The struggle between the German and British navies was called the Battle of the Atlantic. It was the longest battle of World War II, lasting from 1939 to 1945.

In the early years the U-boats nearly won the battle and more ships were sunk than could be built to replace them. In total, 2,500 ships were sunk. Then the navy got detecting systems called **SONAR** and **RADAR**, making it easier to find the enemy underwater (picture ①). Aircraft were designed with a longer range, so they could also help to protect the convoys by spotting the U-boats and even bombing them.

Rationing

As there were limited supplies of food and other essentials, the government decided that the fairest thing was to give rich and poor the same amount. They did this by rationing food and other items.

The ships that crossed the Atlantic during the war could only carry the most essential foods, such as flour for bread and sugar for preserving fruits. Most foods that had once been imported soon vanished completely from the grocer's shelves. There were, for example, few oranges and no bananas at all for six years. Tea and coffee were thought of as essential foods. Milk was concentrated and put in cans, so was beef – it became corned beef, while concentrated pork became spam.

Rationing

Because there was less food coming in to the country the government decided to give everyone the same fair share of the scarce resources – whether they were rich or poor. The scheme was called **RATIONING**, and food that was rationed was only available through coupons in a specially issued ration book (picture ①).

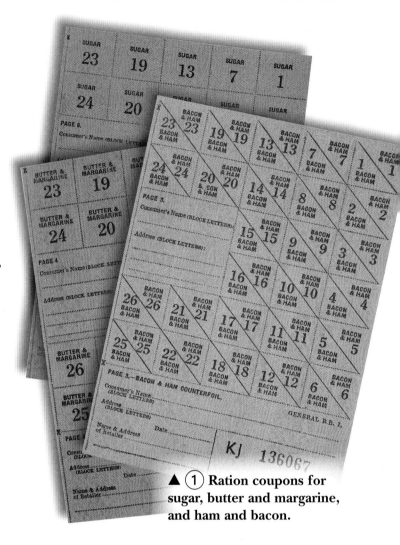

▲ ① Ration coupons for sugar, butter and margarine, and ham and bacon.

Radio broadcasts told people of changes to the rations.

Everyone took part in rationing – even the Royal Family.

Ration books had to be renewed and new ones issued every Summer.

Everyone had to register with their local shop and the shopkeeper was then given enough food for their registered customers by the Ministry of Food.

If the shop where people were registered happened to be bombed they had to register with another shop in order to use their ration book and buy their goods.

WHAT DID PEOPLE EAT DURING THE WAR?

DATES ITEMS ARE RATIONED

29 September 1939

National Register set up and Identity Cards issued.

*The amounts given are per person per week unless otherwise stated.

8 January 1940

Rationing begins
Butter: 4oz*

Sugar: 12oz

Bacon: 4oz

March 1940

Meat: 1s. 10d (9p)

July 1940

No more bananas or fruit (except a few oranges for children).

Tea: 2oz

Sugar: 8oz

March 1941

Jam: 8oz

Cheese: 2oz

June 1941

Eggs: 1 fresh egg

Meat: 1s (5p)

December 1941

Milk: 3 pints

(7 pints for young children and expectant mothers)

February 1942

Soap: 1 small tablet (per month)

June 1942

American dried egg powder on sale.

PURE DRIED WHOLE EGGS

July 1942

Sweets and chocolate: 2oz

21 July 1946

Bread: 9oz (per day) (part of which could be taken as flour or cakes)

DATES ITEMS BECOME FREELY AVAILABLE AGAIN

July 1948	Dec 1948	Oct 1952	Feb 1953	Mar 1953	April 1953	Sept 1953	May 1954	June 1954
Bread	Jam	Tea	Sweets	Eggs	Cream	Sugar	Butter, cheese and margarine	Meat and bacon

Weblink: www.CurriculumVisions.com

Much more than just food

It was not just food that was rationed. Clothing and cosmetics had ration books (picture ②), as did soap and washing powder. Coal and gas were also rationed and people were told not to put more than 5 in (13 cm) of water in a bath to save on the use of coal for heating the water.

Because medicines were needed by those fighting, even medicines were in short supply at home.

Rationing grows

In January 1940 butter, bacon and sugar were the first things to be rationed (see page 35). Meat and jam were added in March 1940. Tea, margarine and cooking fats were added in July 1940 and cheese in 1941. Later, rice, condensed milk, breakfast cereals, biscuits and cornflakes were rationed.

Milk was in short supply because the most efficient use of land is to grow crops, not rear animals. Much land that would have been grazed was ploughed up and the number of animals reduced.

Milk was delivered using the traditional horse and cart because petrol was rationed.

▲ ② Clothing coupons.

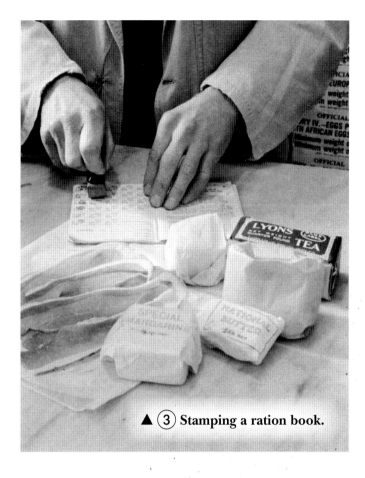

▲ ③ Stamping a ration book.

Queuing

Queuing was an important part of life for women. It took longer to serve customers as ration books had to be stamped, and many items were in short supply anyway (pictures ③ and ④).

If a shop suddenly had unrationed items for sale, the news would sweep around the neighbourhood and long queues would develop outside.

Queuing for food and other goods was so important that people would ignore air-raid sirens and carry on queuing to save losing their place in the queue.

◄ ④ There was very little choice of food. Most of it was called National Butter, National Flour, etc. Only a few items kept their brand names.

What did people eat during the war?

Because Britain cannot produce enough of the things it needs, it has to get them from other countries. In wartime, the amount Britain needed was kept low by rationing.

The Ministry of Food controlled food supplies through rationing. But it had another job. It had to make sure that people understood how to eat healthily because everyone had to work harder than before.

Food facts were published in the newspapers, shown in cinemas and also broadcast on the BBC radio.

Some forms of meat – rabbit, horse and chicken – were not rationed. But lamb, pork and beef were. Offal (liver, heart, kidneys) was never rationed and people could eat tripe (intestines) and pig's feet in jelly!

The range of foods in the war was much smaller than normal. But no-one went hungry and the rations made sure everyone had a healthy diet, with less fat and meat but more vegetables.

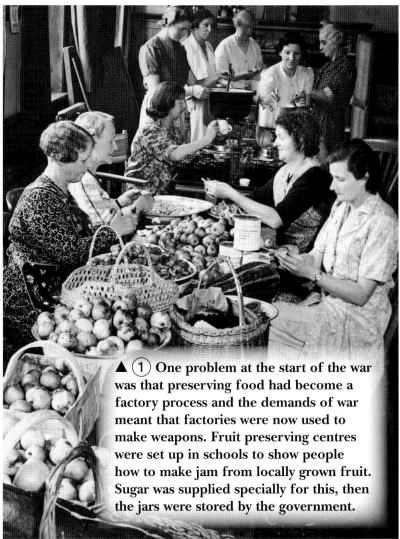

▲ ① **One problem at the start of the war was that preserving food had become a factory process and the demands of war meant that factories were now used to make weapons. Fruit preserving centres were set up in schools to show people how to make jam from locally grown fruit. Sugar was supplied specially for this, then the jars were stored by the government.**

Preserving food

This was a time before fridges were used, so any food grown at home that would not keep naturally had to be preserved in traditional ways, such as drying (meat and fish, eggs and milk), salting (meat, fish and cheese), pickling by putting in vinegar (onions and other vegetables) or boiling in sugar (jams). Many vegetables were best left in the ground until needed (carrots, potatoes, cabbages, etc).

▼ ② National rations: Because of rationing it was vital to know the minimum amount of food that was needed for a person to stay healthy. This was used to work out what the rations should be. You may like to find and weigh out the foods listed here.

A TYPICAL WEEK'S RATION FOR 1 PERSON IN 1942

Bacon and ham	4oz (100g) Meat: To the value of 1s.2d (6p today) (perhaps a pork chop and four sausages). Sausages were not rationed but difficult to get; offal (liver, kidneys, tripe) was originally unrationed but sometimes formed part of the meat ration.
Cheese	2oz (50g) sometimes it went up to 4oz (100g) and even up to 8oz (225g).
Margarine	4oz (100g)
Butter	2oz (50g)
Milk	3 pints (1,800ml) occasionally dropping to 2 pints (1,200ml). Household milk (skimmed or dried) was available: 1 packet per four weeks.
Sugar	8oz (225g)
Jam	1lb (450g) every two months
Tea	2oz (50g) (half a packet or the equivalent of 15 tea bags)
Eggs	1 fresh egg a week if available but often only one every two weeks. Dried eggs: 1 packet every four weeks.
Sweets	12oz (350g) every four weeks

Pea pod soup

Today we might shell fresh peas and throw the pods away. But in the war the pods were used to make a pea pod soup. The pods were washed and placed in a saucepan with a chopped potato, an onion and parsley, or mint if available. It needed lots of salt and pepper to give it flavour (more salt than we would use today). It was brought to the boil and simmered until everything was tender. To make it more substantial, flour was added (about an ounce to each pint of soup). This also gave it a more creamy texture.

Sausage pancakes

Sausages and sausage meat were often easier to get than other kinds of meat. One recipe to vary how they tasted was to cook and mash potatoes, then add sausagemeat and mix it all up. It was then spread over the bottom of a frying pan and fried until golden brown.

If the leftovers from cabbage and other cooked vegetables were added, it was known as BUBBLE AND SQUEAK.

Vegetable oatmeal soup

1oz of margarine, 2 onions chopped, 2 tablespoons of oatmeal, a pint of water, lots of salt and pepper, half a pint of milk and three grated carrots. The oatmeal gave more body to this vegetable soup.

Make the most of it

As rations became smaller, people had to find ways of coping. For example, if potato was added to flour, the flour would go further. Mothers made their own sweets, such as toffee from treacle. Two simple treats were bread and **DRIPPING** and bread and sugar.

If meat coupons were saved and mother was lucky enough to get a roast, she could have the roast on one day, then put some of it into a stew the next day, mince the meat for rissoles, and the remains could be made into **BUBBLE AND SQUEAK** for a fourth day.

Free school milk

From 8 December 1941 all children under the age of 2 were given supplies of free cod liver oil and blackcurrant juice. A small bottle of free milk was given at schools for all children. School dinners also started at this time. These were very important for the poorest people.

◄▼ ① *(Left)* Dig for Victory poster. *(Below)* School children helping to make an allotment in the garden of a bombed house.

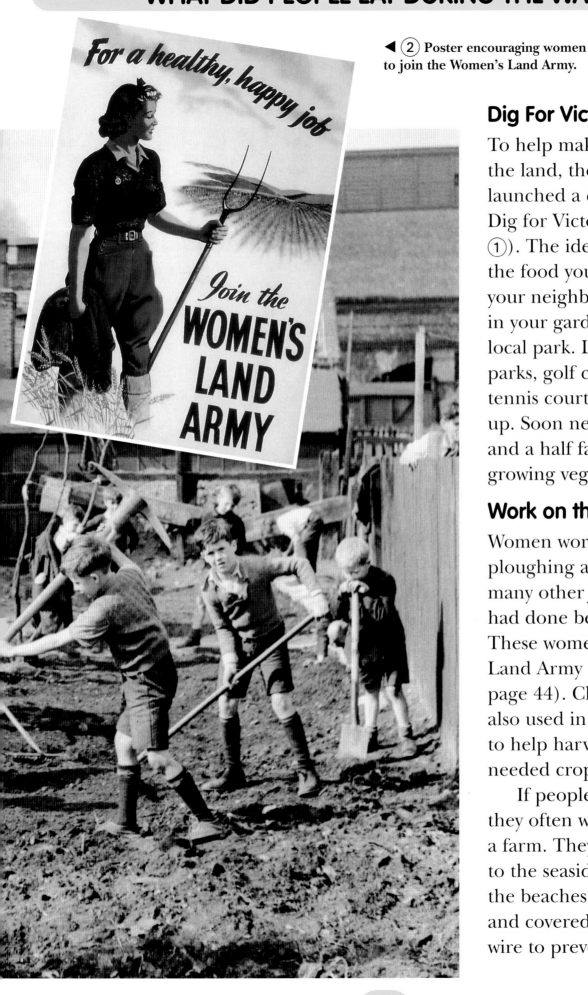

◀ ② Poster encouraging women to join the Women's Land Army.

Dig For Victory

To help make use of all of the land, the government launched a campaign called Dig for Victory (picture ①). The idea was to grow the food you (and perhaps your neighbours) needed in your garden or in your local park. London's royal parks, golf courses and tennis courts were all dug up. Soon nearly a million and a half families were growing vegetables.

Work on the farms

Women worked on farms, ploughing and doing the many other jobs that men had done before the war. These women made up the Land Army (picture ② and page 44). Children were also used in many ways to help harvest the much needed crops.

If people took a holiday, they often went to work on a farm. They could not go to the seaside anyway, for the beaches were closed and covered with barbed wire to prevent invasion.

Wartime Christmas

Christmas was a time of thinking about family members who might be away in the forces and also trying to be imaginative with rationed food and presents.

Christmas was a special time of the year, but it could not be the same as Christmases before the war.

- The blackout meant there were no lights in the shops or on outside Christmas trees (picture ②).
- Rationing meant that it was hard to make a good Christmas meal.
- Shortages meant that it was quite hard to get any kind of present.
- The war meant that many members of a family might be fighting overseas and so would be especially missed at Christmas.
- Evacuation might mean that you were spending Christmas away from your home.

Increased rations

The government tried to help in small ways. For example, in the week before Christmas, the tea ration was doubled and the sugar ration increased to 12 ounces.

▲ ① A party with children dressed as nurses, air-raid wardens or members of the armed forces. Notice all the children have cups of tea.

Practical gifts

People became very inventive about Christmas presents. Mums and dads might give each other a steel helmet or a leather gas mask case.

They might make presents such as by packing an old gas mask container with pouches made from old strips of cloth stuffed with straw. This could be used as a keep-hot box, so they could have a reasonably hot meal for lunch while at work.

▶ ② **Christmas in an Anderson shelter in the garden. Notice the corrugated iron roof. It must have been very cold and damp!**

In the early years of the war children received miniature Red Cross, RAF or naval uniforms (picture ①). New popular annual books appeared, with titles such as the *Blackout Book*.

Soap is most popular gift!

By the middle of the war Christmas gifts were gardening tools, bottling jars, seeds and bags of fertilizer, but the most popular gift was soap. Some parents gave National Savings books with a few savings stamps already added.

If mothers did want extra food at Christmas they had to start saving their ration coupons, or storing away unperishable food, months in advance.

If mums could get the wool, they could knit a pair of gloves as a present, or pull apart an old jumper and reuse the wool. A special treat for Christmas for children may have been a bag of sweets (which were on ration).

Home-made decorations

Many families made their own Christmas decorations by gumming pieces of coloured paper into chains or using any green bushes they could find. The Ministry of Food suggested:

"A Christmassy sparkle is easy to add to sprigs of holly or evergreen for use on puddings. Dip your greenery in a strong solution of Epsom salts. When dry it will be beautifully frosted."

43

In what other ways did the war affect people?

A war is a time of danger, both for the troops fighting it and for the people left at home.

People had curious feelings about the danger of bombing. If you were to have asked many people if they expected to die when the bombing started they would have replied that they never thought about it.

But people did get killed and so all children in cities would have seen more death than anyone today. Bombs might have fallen near to where they lived and they might have lost friends or relatives. Or the bombs might have fallen very close and destroyed part of their house, and even buried them in the rubble.

They may have lost everything they owned, or just been able to collect a few things from their damaged homes.

Worrying about the troops

Most fathers, many brothers and some sisters were in the forces and so there was always the worry that they might be injured or killed in the fighting. For much of the time people did not let themselves think of this, but the only contact was by the occasional **CENSORED LETTER** home.

▲ ① A propaganda poster in support of the women in the forces.

▼ ② Women working on a farm.

It was only when an official letter arrived at the house that some people had to face up to the awful experience of being told that someone they loved had been killed in action.

So people lost a lot that was dear to them, but they had to find the courage to keep going.

▼ ③ During the war, women had to do jobs that men thought only they could do, such as repairing railway tracks.

A new start

Most fathers were away in the forces, and many children did not see their dads for six years – until the end of the war. Mums had to take over many of the jobs that men had done, including working in factories and on farms (pictures ② and ③). They also worked in the forces (picture ①).

Before the war **CLASS** was very important. There were relatively few middle and upper class people and a lot of working class people. There was a big difference between classes, just as there had been in Victorian times.

Because everyone was in the same danger during the war, people were much more willing to help one another. Class began to drop away, for example, in the forces overseas as well as the Home Guard (page 30). The best leader might be from the working class and some of the ordinary soldiers might be upper class.

This made an enormous difference to the way everyone behaved and it would have a great effect on Britain after the war, too, bringing an end to much of the class system. Nothing after the war would be the same again.

Glossary

ABLE-BODIED Those thought fit for active service in the armed forces. People who had illnesses, disabilities or were under 16 or elderly, were not regarded as able-bodied.

ACK-ACK GUNS A common name for anti-aircraft guns. It mimicked the sound of the guns.

AIR RAID A sudden attack by bombing planes.

AIR-RAID WARDEN A person who looked after a neighbourhood, making sure that all residents obeyed the regulations for blackout and so on. They were a kind of special police force.

ALLIES A group of countries who have pledged to fight together.

BILLET The word was originally used to mean the lodging given to troops, often forcibly, during a war. It was extended to mean the lodging of children (also by order) as a result of evacuation.

BUBBLE AND SQUEAK Fried leftovers from previous meals, mainly potato and cabbage.

CENSORED LETTER A letter that has been read by a member of the armed forces with any information that might be of help to an enemy blacked out. This was done during the war so that, if a letter got into the hands of the enemy, it would not give away the position of the person who wrote it.

CLASS The way that people thought of themselves as belonging to different groups based on wealth and upbringing. There were upper, middle and lower (or working) classes. Upper classes were aristocracy, middle classes did not do manual work and received a regular salary, and lower classes did manual work and were paid for what they did (wages). It was a system much used in Victorian times.

CONCENTRATION CAMP A place where people were held without trial in often terrible conditions. In Germany during the Nazi times, concentration camps often included gas chambers where large numbers of people were murdered.

▲ **Boys learning the skills to help them become airforce apprentices.**

DICTATOR A single person who has total power to do what he wishes and who does not have to ask permission of, for example, a parliament.

DRIPPING The fat that dripped off the meat while it roasted. It cooled into a white, and very tasty, fat. It was a very concentrated form of food energy.

FIGHTER PLANES Small, very fast planes equipped only with machine guns. Their job was to shoot down the larger and slower bombers.

MEMORIAL A plaque or stone tablet put up to act as a way of remembering those who lost their lives in the war.

MERCHANT SHIP A ship designed for carrying cargo. Not a fighting vessel.

NAZI The letters in German stand for **NA**tionalso**ZI**alistische Deutsche Arbeiter-Partei: National Socialist German Workers' Party. The leader of the party was Adolf Hitler.

PROPAGANDA A way of changing the meaning of events and actions to suit the purposes of one group of people.

RADAR The letters stand for **RA**(dio) **D**(etection) **A**(nd) **R**(anging). A method of determining the location and speed of an object. Radar works by transmitting signals and measuring the time it takes for them to bounce off the targeted object and return.

RATION/RATIONING A fixed portion of food, coal, clothes, etc, allotted to civilians in times of scarcity.

SONAR The letters stand for **SO**(und) **NA**(vigation and) **R**(anging). It was a measuring instrument that sent out a sound (called a 'ping') in water and measured distances in terms of the time for the echo of the ping to return.

TORPEDO An underwater missile, launched from a submarine.

Index